D1535989

THE $7.50 BUNNY THAT CHANGED THE WORLD

**WRITTEN AND WITH PHOTOGRAPHS
BY GRETTA PARKER**

Published in the United States by BQB Publishing
(Boutique of Quality Books Publishing Company)
www.bqbpublishing.com

Printed in the United States of America

978-1-937084-64-6 (h)
978-1-937084-71-4 (p)
978-1-937084-72-1 (e)

Library of Congress Control Number: 2012944844

Book design by Robin Krauss, www.lindendesign.biz

FOREWORD AND DEDICATION

I would not have spent $30,000 on college if I had known my greatest teacher would cost me $7.50. His name was Flopsy Parker. He taught me a lot of things, but his most valuable lesson was that sometimes the greatest gifts are the ones other people discard.

In life, people can choose their journeys. In my case, mine chose me. I walked into Guildford County shelter on a rainy Sunday

afternoon with the intention of donating after seeing a newscast on rabbits that were abandoned after Easter. I left with a crazy-haired white rabbit that would lead me on the greatest journey of my life. I did not pick him that day. He picked me.

He saw my strengths before I did, and I used them all as I began to want to help rabbits. He forced me to grow, but, most importantly, he taught me to love without fear. People told me I was crazy for starting a Facebook page for him, but I did not care. I went on to start a nonprofit called Baskets for Bunnies, Inc., and to start a toy-donation program called Toys for Hops, because Flopsy taught me to care for the unwanted rabbits of the world as if they were my own. At the height of our work together, my best friend, my greatest teacher, and my son left me to go back to heaven. I had always known Flopsy was an angel. I guess it was just time for him to go home. My heart was broken, but there were still rabbits who needed my help.

I received close to three thousand emails in the days following his death. The emails told stories of adoption and how Flopsy had affected people's lives, and they said how much he was missed. They gave me strength. Flopsy was still leading me even though he was not physically with me. I owe every opportunity during the last two years to him. Being his mom was the greatest thing I have ever done, and it is a privilege to share images from his life in this book. His photographs never needed editing or special lighting, because Flopsy always wore his soul on the outside. *The $7.50 Bunny That Changed the World* is a true account of his life and is dedicated to all the rabbits around the world in rescues and shelters today waiting for their forever homes.

One fall day, Marshmallow and his family took a drive. The leaves danced off the car windows as they drove. He hoped he wasn't going to the veterinarian again. He hated getting his toenails trimmed. His family always called them "pawdicures," but he knew better. Fancy names couldn't fool him.

He heard the tires of the car make a crunchy noise. This was the same sound they made when his family visited his grammie's house. He thought he was wrong about the vet's office. *They're surprising me with a day in the country*, he thought. He could not wait to put on his harness and leash and go exploring. He hoped the geese would be there, because he liked to watch them.

He waited patiently, excited to breathe the cool, crisp country air as they pulled into a gravel driveway. The car stopped. Usually, everyone jumped out of the car and started to unpack it. This time, his family sat quietly in the car. Then his dad unfastened his seatbelt, came around to the back seat, and unloaded Marshmallow from the car. Marshmallow looked back at his mom and her son. They would not look his way. He wondered why.

His dad carried him into a brick building. Marshmallow heard all kinds of animals as soon as his dad opened the door. The meows and barks were sad, not excited. He sniffed the air. This place did not smell like the veterinarian's office or his grammie's house. There were dogs barking, pet carriers strewn about the place, and people sitting around. So he told himself that this must be the veterinarian's office. He wondered where the nice nurse who always greeted them was.

His dad set his cage on the floor and talked to a person behind a counter. After a few minutes, his dad bent down and looked into his cage.

"Sorry, little man," he said. Then he stood up and walked away.

Where is he going? Marshmallow thought. He watched his dad walk out the door. Marshmallow had never been left alone before.

Marshmallow thought, *He'll be right back. He probably forgot something.* So Marshmallow waited patiently. Five minutes turned into twenty, and his dad did not come back. Marshmallow watched the light sky outside the glass door turn darker. He watched the people in the lobby leave. He found himself alone with other animals that looked as confused as he was.

"Are we at summer camp?" a brown-and-tan puppy in a gray carrier asked. Marshmallow watched the animals in the other cages exchange looks. He started to panic as he watched a one-eyed ferret shake its head. Marshmallow thought there was something terribly wrong with this place where his family had left him.

Someone lifted his cage and carried him to

a table in the back of the big room. Once he was above the floor, he could see animals in carriers all over the floor. They had all been dropped off there on this most beautiful of fall days.

My days of hiding under beds have come to an end, he thought. This wasn't the veterinarian's office. This was an animal shelter. From the sad faces of the other orphaned animals, Marshmallow knew his family wasn't coming back. He wondered what he had done wrong.

That night, he listened to the sad howls, barks, and meows of the other residents. Marshmallow hid as far down in his cage as he could. This was not his warm, quiet room at home. He had no fluffy towels, only a small scrap of denim in the bottom of his cage. There were no toys or hay, just some pellets and a yellowed water bottle.

The next day, the lobby was busy again. He wiggled his nose and sat at the edge of his cage. Each time the door opened, he hoped to see his dad's face.

Every day, people glanced at him, making noises and sometimes petting him, but no one took him home. He missed hugs the most.

Every day, he sat in his cage in the shelter's lobby, hoping someone would want him. No one came. He was always happy when the other animals found their forever homes, but he also felt a little jealous and wondered what they were having for dinner. His mom used to give him cilantro in the evenings. He had not seen anything green in days. The people who gave him dinner seemed so busy, because they had so many animals to feed. He wished just one would sit and talk to him until he fell asleep.

The days and nights blurred together. Until everything changed.

One rainy day, the front door opened, and a lady with dark hair stepped into the lobby. She stood in line, waiting to talk to the person behind the counter. As she waited, she happened to look over at Marshmallow.

She stared at him. He stared back. Her hair was wet from the rain outside. It was funny how it stuck to her face like she had noodles on her head.

She kept staring. Then she walked over, opened the cage, and petted him very gently. But then she shut the cage, just like everyone else, and went back to her place in line.

When it was her turn, she talked to the person behind the counter. And then, something different happened. The lady and the person behind the counter were walking toward Marshmallow with a cardboard carrier.

The next thing he knew, Marshmallow was safely inside the dark carrier. He could smell the rain as she carried him outside. He was so scared when the lady said they were going for a ride. She continued to talk to him softly as they drove. After a few minutes, he heard her get out of the car. When she came back, she loaded up the back seat beside Marshmallow with a whole bunch of stuff. The lady drove a few minutes more. This time, when she stopped and got out, she took Marshmallow with her.

A door closed and the sounds of the rain stopped, so he knew he was inside. It smelled different from the shelter, almost like his old home.

And then, the cardboard carrier opened. The lady smiled at him and gently lifted him out. She placed him in a large pen with a soft rug, wooden toys to chew, and hay to eat. It was quiet. He looked around, but he was too tired to explore. The lady left him alone, and he fell asleep.

He woke the next morning to rays of sunshine

coming through a window. The lady was right beside him, watching him. She gave him some parsley and cilantro.

She said, "Are you hungry, Flopsy?"

Flopsy? Who is Flopsy? He was confused. He missed his family. He felt sad. And now he was being called strange names.

The nice lady opened the cage and lifted him up onto a bed. She let him hop around on the fluffy bedspread. He sat with her while she watched television.

She petted his head, and she laughed as he hopped around. This is better than the shelter, he told himself. It was quiet here, and it was warm.

She gave him a new litter box and food dish. He flipped both of them. He discovered that the lady would come see him every time that he did this. She always brought something called a Shop-Vac with her too. He began to flip the litter boxes daily. It seemed to entertain the human.

Every day, the lady let him play on the bed. And every day, she called him Flopsy. He liked his new name, but he wondered if someday she too would stop wanting him. One day when she came home from work, she had a very big surprise for him.

"I got you a computer today," she said proudly. He watched with curiosity as she set it up on the table.

"We are going to start you a Facebook page

and teach other people about rabbits in shelters." She wiggled her nose at him as she took him out of his enclosure. He stared at the bright screen. He tilted his head, trying to make sense of what she meant.

She bought a new camera the next day and started taking his picture. He decided pictures were fun. He would pose with a silly look sometimes. Other times, he would pose like the king of his castle.

One day, she took him out onto the patio and took some black-and-white photos. *I'm looking pretty dapper in this harness*, he thought to himself. The lady leaned down and whispered, "You are going to be the $7.50 bunny that changes the world. You are very special, Flopsy Parker."

My mom is pretty cool, he thought. Errrrrr . . . wait . . . I just called her mom. Unlike his old family, who spent less and less time with him, the lady spent more and more time with him. He began to stop thinking of her as "the lady" and began thinking of her more as "mom." Flopsy began to feel that this lady would never stop wanting him. And he was right.

She posted his pictures and made posters for his Facebook page, all talking about adoption. He made more and more friends every day. His mom would let him read the emails and posts from people all over the world. He was no longer the bunny from the shelter. He was the bunny who had found his forever home. He began to take his new job of spokesbunny for adoption very seriously. He even got a

catchphrase on Facebook, because his mom always posted all of his mischief online.

Every time he flipped his food dish or litter box, his mom would update his status and write, "Can't be Tamed." If he misbehaved, she posted it. If he woke her up, she posted it. People found his bad behavior funny, and because Flopsy liked to flip things, he kept everyone laughing.

People began to share his page, and more and more people started to follow the funny little Facebook rabbit. More importantly, people also saw that wonderful rabbits end up in shelters and rescues every day around the world, and they began to want to adopt rabbits into their families.

Just when he thought his life could not get

any better, his mom brought home a tiny, brown bunny with big brown eyes. She named her Isabella.

"You have pretty eyes," Flopsy muttered. She was so pretty and tiny that he was taken aback. *I'm going to be the best big brother*, he told himself.

"Who are you?" she questioned, looking around her new surroundings.

"I am Flopsy Parker. I am a spokesbunny," he told her proudly.

"I have no idea what that is," she said, almost sadly. He felt sorry for her, because he could tell by the sadness that danced across her beautiful eyes that her family had left her behind too.

"It's okay. Our new mom is very nice. You will get your own Facebook page here, and you can make all kinds of new friends," he boasted. *I'm already getting this big brother thing down*, he thought to himself.

"I just want to sleep. I am tired," she said meekly, as she snuggled down into the rug on the floor. He watched her drift off.

"I will always take care of you," he whispered, gently grooming her fur. From that moment on, they became bonded as brother and sister. Flopsy kept his promise.

Flopsy taught Bella to use the litter box. At mealtime, he let her eat first. They played tag. She groomed his fur. They slept side-by-side, ate together, and played together for hours. He loved the crinkle tunnel that made fun noises. She was the perfect baby sister.

Now, both of them were spokesbunnies for other bunnies who did not have homes. Their mom took their photos together and made adoption posters for the Internet. People loved their photos. Flopsy made new friends online every day who told him he was very special. He liked when his mom shared facts about bunnies. For example, people believe that rabbits should eat carrots, but the truth is that hay is healthier. And some rabbits need dental care to be healthy, just like people do. The most important lesson his mom posted explained that families should research an animal's care needs before bringing it into their homes.

"Flopsy, it was not your fault you ended up in a shelter. It was because your old family didn't feel they were ready to take care of you for ten years. Bunnies are a commitment, and it takes the right research for families to find a pet suited to their lifestyles," she said to him one night as she tucked him into his warm fleece. *She's right. It's not my fault*, he thought as he nestled into his blanket.

That summer, his mom wasn't home as much. But she had a big surprise for them. She had worked a lot of extra hours, and she used the extra money to start a nonprofit called Baskets for Bunnies, Inc. She told Flopsy and Bella that they were going to help raise money for rabbit rescues. Bella and Flopsy were so excited that they ran through their crinkle tunnel to celebrate. Flopsy flipped his litter box just because. His mom just shook her head.

They started a program called Toys for Hops that fall, and they provided free rabbit toys to shelters all over the world. His mom wanted every bunny to have the life that Flopsy and Bella had. Flopsy did, too, because in the last year, his life had become amazing.

A pet toy company called Pet Rabbit Toys agreed to help them. Using his Facebook page, Flopsy set out to obtain donations and toys for bunnies who needed them. He wanted to get two thousand toys by Christmas. He dressed up like Santa and proclaimed himself Santa Paws.

He asked all of his Facebook friends to

help him. His mom made him posters, and people sent in pictures of their bunnies to use as well. People shared, and shared, and shared some more. By December 20, the two thousand toys were raised and shipped to rescues all over the United States.

Flopsy finally felt like he had a new mom and a forever family. Everyone showered him and Bella with love. He could not believe it. *My life is perfect*, he thought gladly to himself. He had found his true forever home.

Then, one morning just before Christmas, Flopsy felt very tired. He thought it must have been all the help he gave for Toys for Hops. He felt better that night and harassed his baby sister until she was annoyed. Flopsy watched his mom pack toys as he fell asleep.

By Christmas, he was feeling more tired every day. He did not have his normal energy to play.

"What's wrong, Flopsy?" Bella asked one day. Her big eyes were full of concern.

"Nothing, just didn't sleep well, kind of tired," he said softly. He didn't tell her that he had seen a soft white image of a beautiful lady in his dream the day before. She was not scary but was instead peaceful.

"Okay, well, that litter box isn't going to flip itself, and I haven't seen Mom use the Shop-Vac all day. She is going to know something is wrong." Bella was acting sassy, but Flopsy could tell she was really worried.

The following day, his mom gave them breakfast and picked him up.

"Are you feeling okay, funny bunny?" she asked. He looked at her and nodded his head. She looked into his eyes, then kissed him on the head, whispering, "I love you, funny bunny." On this cold winter day, his sister Bella was in the mood to play, but he was just too tired.

That night, he ate his dinner, feeling more tired than ever. Afterward, he lay down to sleep. He felt as if he had taken a long nap, but unlike the other times, he could not wake up, even though he could feel Bella grooming him and hear her calling his name more and more frantically. He could see the beautiful lady in white that he had seen before. He felt her gently pulling him to her. He did not feel scared as he heard his mother crying. The brightness surrounding the beautiful lady made him feel safe.

"Hello," he said. His voice sounded so small here. This was the most beautiful place he had ever seen. As his eyes began to focus on the bright light, he could see other animals playing on a large rainbow bridge. Unlike the sad animals at the shelter, these animals all sounded happy.

A soft voice said, "Hello, little one. We have been expecting you."

"Me?" Flopsy asked.

"Yes," the voice replied.

"Where am I, and why is my mom so sad?" Flopsy wondered why he couldn't wake up. He wanted to go home.

The voice said, "She is sad because she had to say goodbye to you today. She will be fine. She will eventually learn why you had to come here even though it does not make sense to her right now."

"You mean I can't go home?" Flopsy thought maybe he should be scared, but the voice soothed him.

"Flopsy, you were never meant to live on Earth very long. You were always a special little bunny. Your mom saw that in you when she made you the Facebook page. You always took beautiful pictures, and you have always worn your very special soul on the outside. All people had to do was look at you to see how truly special you are," the voice explained. "You're an angel now. You are the Angel of Bunny Adoptions, and your purpose was always to guide families to find their perfect rescue bunny."

"Are you sure my mom and sister will be okay if I stay here?" Flopsy asked, still sensing his mother's sadness.

"Yes," said the voice. "Your mom cannot see it now, but she will understand why you had to go so soon." Flopsy was worried about his mom, but he knew he could trust the voice. That night, while his mom slept, he whispered in her ear that she should open her home to other bunnies who need her.

Flopsy was filled with peace as he saw his

mom and sister adopt two bunnies named Bun Jovi and Puffy P the following week. Bella followed the litter box lessons he had given her, and she showed the others how to use the litter box and how to toss it over five minutes later.

He saw his mom cry less and less. He could still feel her in his heart as she felt him in hers. He would always be her son. She came to understand that, really, it was not her who had chosen him in the animal shelter that day, but he that had chosen her. He started the journey with her, but she would have to finish it alone. And she did. She built the Flopsy Parker Memorial Sanctuary in his memory that same year.

His mom and Bella began to take in

misunderstood rabbits from shelters. The first was named Stanley. He had behavioral issues, according to his former family. Flopsy smiled when he saw Stanley with his mom. He knew that she soon would see that he was really an artist.

The second was Snicklefritz, a former magician's rabbit who was in his elder years. Flopsy's mom decided Snicklefritz needed a home to retire to. One by one, Flopsy guided each bunny to the sanctuary. His mom began to understand that even though he had left her physically, they would always continue their work together. She truly understood how lucky she had been to have lived with a real angel.

From then on, Flopsy helped families find

their way to shelters that rescue and adopt bunnies into loving homes around the world. He watches over the frightened ones who are still waiting. He casually whispers into their ears, "The greatest gifts are sometimes the ones other people discard."